World
FLAGS

CONTENTS

FLAGS of the WORLD

Every country in the World
has a flag.

Flags come in many shapes
and sizes.

There are many different coloured flags and some have symbols with a special meaning.

5

FLAGS of EUROPE

ICELAND

UNITED KINGDOM

NETHE'

IRELAND

This map shows the
flag for each country
in Europe.

BELGIUM

LUXEM

FRANCE

SWITZ

ANDORRA

M

PORTUGAL

SPAIN

6

FLAG COLOURS

 CZECH REPUBLIC

 UNITED KINGDOM

 FRANCE

 SLOVENIA

 LUXEMBOURG

 SLOVAKIA

 NETHERLANDS

 NORWAY

 DENMARK

 FINLAND

 GREECE

 SWITZERLAND

All these flags have three
colours.
They are red, white and blue.

These flags have only two
colours. Some are blue and
white and some are red and
white.

FLAGS of NORTH AMERICA

This map shows the flag for each country in North America. The flag of the USA is made up of stars and stripes. The Canadian flag shows the national emblem. This is a maple leaf.

GREENLAND
(Denmark)

CANADA

UNITED STATES
OF AMERICA

MEXICO

BELIZE

GUATEMALA

HONDU

EL SALVADOR

NICAR

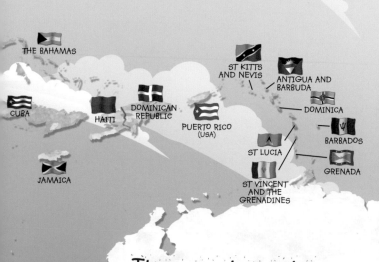

THE BAHAMAS

ST KITTS AND NEVIS

ANTIGUA AND BARBUDA

CUBA

HAITI

DOMINICAN REPUBLIC

PUERTO RICO (USA)

DOMINICA

BARBADOS

ST LUCIA

GRENADA

JAMAICA

ST VINCENT AND THE GRENADINES

RICA

PANAMA

This map shows the flag for each country in Central America and the Caribbean.

STRIPES and STARS

 THE BAHAMAS

 NICARAGUA

 BARBADOS

 HONDURAS

 COSTA RICA

 HAITI

 CUBA

 EL SALVADOR

 PANAMA

 PUERTO RICO

 GRENADA

 ST KITTS AND NEVIS

The colours on flags are often shown as stripes. Many of these flags have blue and white stripes.

These flags have stars. Some flags have only one star and some have many stars.

FLAGS of SOUTH AMERICA

This map shows the flag for each country in South America.

TRINIDAD
& TOBAGO

VENEZUELA

GUYANA
SURINAME
FRENCH
GUIANA

COLOMBIA

JADOR

PERU

BRAZIL

BOLIVIA

PARAGUAY

CHILE

ARGENTINA   URUGUAY

17

RED, YELLOW and WHITE

 ECUADOR

 BOLIVIA

 COLOMBIA

 GUYANA

 VENEZUELA

 SURINAME

 BRAZIL

 ARGENTINA

 TRINIDAD & TOBAGO

 CHILE

 URUGUAY

 PARAGUAY

These flags have the colours
red and yellow.

White shapes appear
on all of these flags.

FLAGS of AFRICA

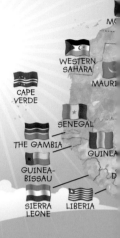

MO...

WESTERN
SAHARA

MAURI...

CAPE
VERDE

SENEGAL

THE GAMBIA

GUINEA

GUINEA-
BISSAU

D...

SIERRA
LEONE

LIBERIA

This map shows the flag for each country in Africa.

ONE, TWO, THREE

 LIBYA

 ZAMBIA

 TUNISIA

 REPUBLIC OF SOUTH AFRICA

 SOMALIA

 KENYA

 NIGERIA

 ETHIOPIA

 MOROCCO

Sometimes flags have only one or two colours. Many flags have lots of colours.

FLAGS of ASIA

CYPRUS

TURKEY

GEORGIA

LEBANON

ISRAEL

SYRIA

ARMENIA

AZERBAIJAN

UZBEKISTAN

KAZAKHSTAN

MONG

RUSSIAN
FEDERATION

JORDAN

IRAQ

KUWAIT

IRAN

TURKMENISTAN

KYRGYZSTAN

TAJIKISTAN

AFGHANISTAN

BAHRAIN

SAUDI ARABIA

QATAR

UNITED ARAB
EMIRATES

PAKISTAN

NEPAL

BHUTAN

C

YEMEN

OMAN

INDIA

BANGLADESH

MYANMA
(BURMA)

SRI LANKA

THAI

MALDIVES

24

NORTH KOREA

JAPAN

SOUTH KOREA

TAIWAN

PALAU

PHILIPPINES

OIA

TNAM

BRUNEI

AYSIA

APORE

INDONESIA

EAST TIMOR

This map shows
the flag for each
country in Asia.

25

MOON, SUN and STARS

 TURKEY

 MALAYSIA

 PAKISTAN

 PHILIPPINES

 SINGAPORE

 TURKMENIS

 CHINA

 JORDAN

 IRAQ

 SYRIA

Some flags show a symbol of a crescent moon, the sun or the stars.

FLAGS of OCEANIA

INDONESIA

PAPUA NEW GUINEA

AUSTRALIA

NAURU

KIRIBATI

ON
DS

TUVALU

SAMOA

U

FIJI

TONGA

FRENCH
POLYNESIA

This map shows the
flag for each country
in Oceania.

EW
AND

RED, WHITE and BLUE

 AUSTRALIA

 TONGA

 NEW ZEALAND

 SAMOA

 PAPUA NEW GUINEA

 KIRIBATI

 FIJI

 SOLOMON ISLANDS

 TUVALU